Isaac Asimov's

21st Century

Library of the Universe

The Solar System

Mars

BY ISAAC ASIMOV

WITH REVISIONS AND UPDATING BY RICHARD HANTULA

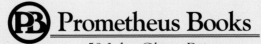

Prometheus Books

59 John Glenn Drive
Amherst, New York 14228-2197

Published 2003 by Prometheus Books

Inquiries should be addressed to
Prometheus Books, 59 John Glenn Drive, Amherst, New York 14228-2197
VOICE: 716-691-0133, ext. 207; FAX: 716-564-2711
WWW.PROMETHEUSBOOKS.COM

Library of Congress Cataloging-in-Publication Data

Asimov, Isaac, 1920-1992.
    Mars / by Isaac Asimov.
       p. cm. — (Isaac Asimov's 21st century library of the universe. Solar system)
    Originally published: Milwaukee, WI: Gareth Stevens Pub., 2002.
    Includes bibliographical references and index.
    ISBN 1-59102-124-3 (alk. paper)
    1. Mars (Planet)—Juvenile literature. I. Title. II. Series: Asimov, Isaac, 1920- Isaac Asimov's 21st century library of the universe. Solar system.
  QB641.A755 2003
  523.43—dc21   2003046621

This revised and updated edition first published in 2002 by
Gareth Stevens Publishing
A World Almanac Education Group Company
330 West Olive Street, Suite 100
Milwaukee, WI 53212 USA

Original edition published in 1988 by Gareth Stevens, Inc. under the title *Mars: Our Mysterious Neighbor.*
Second edition published in 1994 by Gareth Stevens, Inc. under the title *The Red Planet: Mars.*
Text © 2002 by Nightfall, Inc. End matter and revisions © 2002 by Gareth Stevens, Inc.

Series editor: Betsy Rasmussen
Cover design and layout adaptation: Melissa Valuch
Picture research: Kathy Keller
Additional picture research: Diane Laska-Swanke
Artwork commissioning: Kathy Keller and Laurie Shock
Production director: Susan Ashley

The editors at Gareth Stevens Publishing have selected science author Richard Hantula to bring this classic series of young people's information books up to date. Richard Hantula has written and edited books and articles on science and technology for more than two decades. He was the senior U.S. editor for the *Macmillan Encyclopedia of Science.*

In addition to Hantula's contribution to this most recent edition, the editors would like to acknowledge the participation of two noted science authors, Greg Walz-Chojnacki and Francis Reddy, as contributors to earlier editions of this work.

Printed in the United States of America

1 2 3 4 5 6 7 8 9 06 05 04 03

Contents

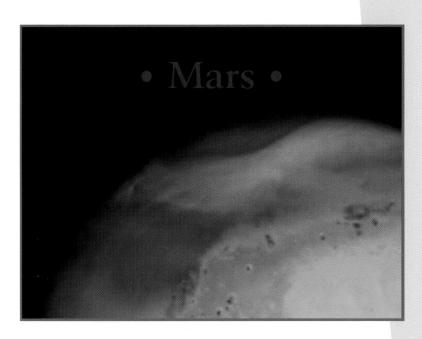

• Mars •

We live in an enormously large place – the Universe. It is only natural that we would want to understand this place, so scientists and engineers have developed instruments and spacecrafts that have told us far more about the Universe than we could possibly imagine.

We have seen planets up close, and spacecrafts have even landed on some. We have learned about quasars and pulsars, supernovas and colliding galaxies, and black holes and dark matter. We have gathered amazing data about how the Universe may have come into being and how it may end. Nothing could be more astonishing.

Thousands of years ago, people watched the sky and noticed that certain bright stars shifted position from night to night. The ancient Greeks called them "wandering stars." From the Greek word for wandering, we get our English word "planet." One planet has a reddish color – almost the color of blood – and it was given the name of the ancient Roman god of war, Mars. Scientists have discovered many fascinating things about the planet Mars.

Is There Life on Mars?

If we leave Earth, heading away from the Sun, Mars is the first planet we see. We know quite a bit about our neighbor. We know that Mars is smaller than Earth. Mars is only $1/2$ as wide as Earth, and it has only a little more than $1/10$ Earth's mass. Mars turns, or rotates, once every $24 1/2$ hours. Its axis is tipped so that it has seasons like Earth's.

Mars is colder than Earth, though, because it is farther from the Sun. It has ice caps at both poles. Of all the planets in our Solar System, Mars is in some ways the one most like Earth. In the past, people wondered whether or not there were living creatures on Mars. If so, what were they like? This was the big mystery of Mars.

Computers combined many images from the *Viking Orbiter* probe to create this view of Mars as seen from the window of a spacecraft 1,500 miles (2,500 kilometers) above the Red Planet. Near the center is the crater Schiaparelli, which is about 280 miles (450 km) across. Frost fills craters and dusts the landscape at lower right.

An artist's depiction of the *Mars Odyssey* spacecraft firing its engine upon reaching Mars in October 2001.

Martian Canals

We know that living creatures would have a difficult time surviving on Mars. Early astronomers could tell that Mars had only a thin atmosphere, very little water, and was probably made up of a large desert. In 1877, however, narrow, dark markings were seen on Mars. These were studied by U.S. astronomer Percival Lowell. He thought they were canals, dug by intelligent Martians to bring water from the ice caps at the poles to the desert areas on the rest of the planet. Lowell wrote several books on the subject, and, for a while, many people were sure there was intelligent life on Mars.

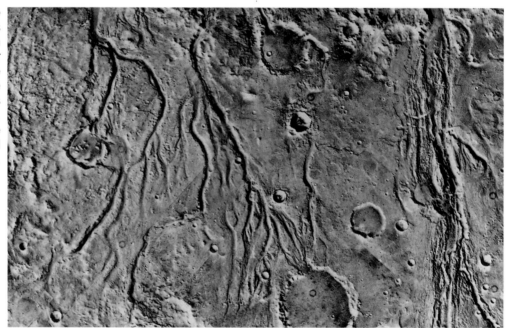

Right: These channels on Mars may have been carved by water long ago. They are not, however, the same as the ones seen by Lowell, which may have been optical illusions.

Calling all Martians!

People were once so sure Mars had intelligent beings on it that ways were invented to send messages there. One scientist suggested that huge triangles and squares be dug in Siberia, filled with oil, and set on fire at night. The idea was that the Martians would see these fires through their telescopes, and then they might arrange something for us to see in return. In 1938, the actor Orson Welles presented a fictional radio play in which Martians were said to be invading New Jersey. He frightened hundreds of listeners who got into their cars and drove away to escape the Martians — who really did not exist.

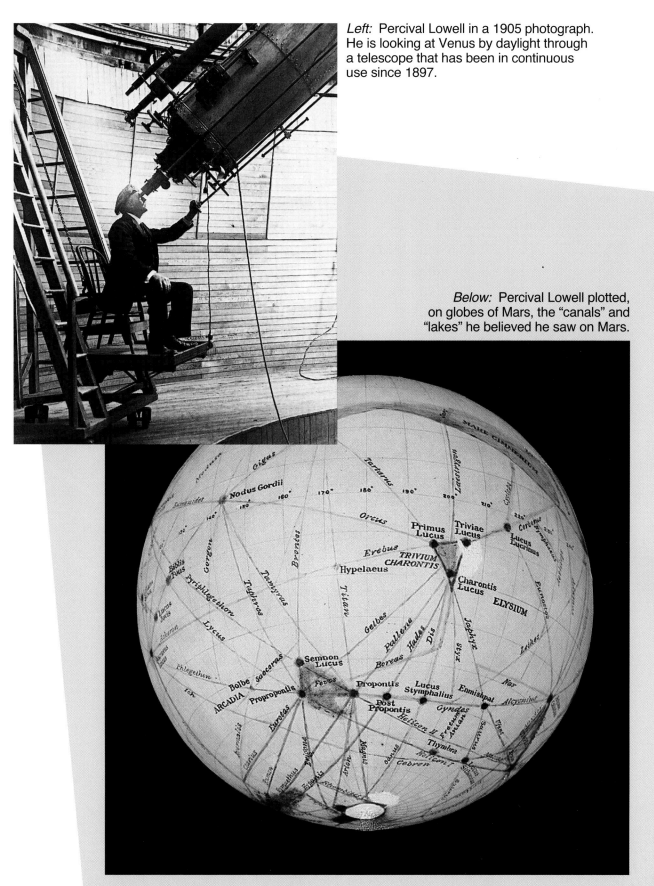

Left: Percival Lowell in a 1905 photograph. He is looking at Venus by daylight through a telescope that has been in continuous use since 1897.

Below: Percival Lowell plotted, on globes of Mars, the "canals" and "lakes" he believed he saw on Mars.

As the *Mariner 4* space probe passed Mars, its television camera took pictures. These pictures were stored on tape and beamed back to Earth. Each picture took about eight hours to reconstruct, or play back, from the radio transmission. The entire transmission lasted over seven days.

A Dead World

For many years, people wondered about the possibility of life on Mars. When scientists sent rockets to Mars, it seemed we would finally get some answers. In 1964, the *Mariner 4* probe was sent to Mars. In July 1965, this probe passed within 6,000 miles (9,600 km) of the planet and took 19 close-up photographs that it beamed back to Earth. These photographs showed craters on Mars like those on the Moon. Mars's atmosphere turned out to be only $1/100$ as thick as Earth's. No sign of any canals was found. Mars seemed to be a dead world.

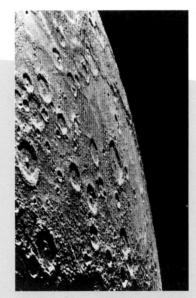

Above: The Moonlike southern region of Mars. The Red Planet looks barren, but many scientists are still searching for evidence of life there.

Another Look

Another Mars probe, *Mariner 9*, reached Mars in 1971. It went into orbit around Mars and took several photographs. It mapped almost the entire planet and found no canals. The photos showed that the straight, dark lines thought to be canals were just illusions. The photos also showed many craters and flat areas with extinct volcanoes. One of these volcanoes, Olympus Mons, was far larger than any volcano on Earth. The pictures also showed a huge canyon, named Valles Marineris, that was far larger than our own Grand Canyon. Mars's surface proved to be much more interesting than that of our Moon.

Right: Olympus Mons, Mars's biggest extinct volcano, is the largest known volcano in the Solar System. A *Viking* probe took this false-color image.

Mars — fooling the pros

Why did Percival Lowell see canals on Mars when there were none to see? He was a good astronomer with excellent telescopes. He worked on high ground in Arizona where the air was very clear. It is possible that he could just barely see little dark patches on Mars. His eyes, not knowing what to make of the patches, saw them as straight lines. During a scientific experiment, children looked at distant circles with little dark patches. The children saw straight lines — an optical illusion. Maybe that is what Lowell experienced.

Mars is famous for its dust storms. Here is what a dust storm might look like from the floor of Valles Marineris.

Above: Over 2,500 miles (4,000 km) long and up to 5 miles (8 km) deep, the Valles Marineris dwarfs any canyon system on Earth. Earth's entire Grand Canyon would fit into the little box pictured here. The 3 dark spots are Martian volcanoes. The crater of the bottom volcano, named Arsia Mons, is filled with fog.

11

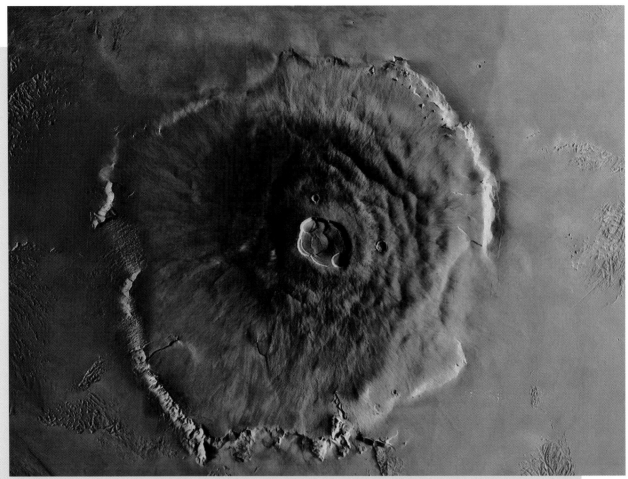

Above: At its base, the extinct volcano Olympus Mons is over 300 miles (500 km) across. It is about 16 miles (25 km) high — nearly 3 times higher than the tallest mountain on Earth.

Left: The back row shows mountain peaks on Mars. Olympus Mons *(back, right)* is 82,000 feet (25,000 m) high. The center row of mountains *(left to right)* are Earth's Mt. Everest (29,035 feet/8,850 m), Mt. Rainier (14,410 feet/4,392 m), and Mont Blanc (15,771 feet/ 4,807 m). In the front row are Earth's Mt. Fuji (12,388 feet/ 3,776 m) and Mt. Saint Helens (8,365 feet/ 2,550 m).

Probing Mars

Two Mars probes, *Viking 1* and *Viking 2*, successfully put landers on the Martian surface in 1976. A part of the mission was to analyze the atmosphere of the red planet. It was found to be about 95 percent carbon dioxide, and most of the rest is nitrogen and argon. This means that the Martian atmosphere has almost no oxygen in it. What is more, the Martian surface is generally as cold or colder than Antarctica, so any water on Mars must be frozen.

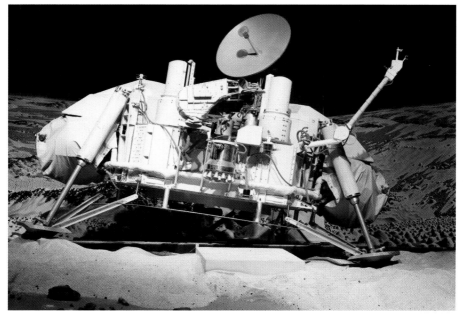

Above: A model of the *Viking* lander. The front footpad of this model rests on a rock, as the actual lander did on Mars. As a result, cameras in the lander showed the Martian horizon as sloped. In fact, it is nearly perfectly level.

More strange markings

Space probes have discovered strange markings on Mars. These markings look like dry river channels that run crookedly across the surface as real rivers would. Smaller channels run into larger ones just as smaller rivers run into larger ones on Earth. It seems very likely that at one time in the past, Mars had water that formed rivers and, perhaps, lakes. It also seems likely that some of that water is still on Mars, lying frozen below the surface. If Mars once had water, was the atmosphere thicker then and was there life on Mars then? Scientists do not know.

No Life as We Know It

The *Viking* probes took photographs of Mars's surface and tested the Martian soil. If the soil contained microscopic forms of life, the tests would show the presence of chemical changes. The probes scooped up soil and tested it in three different ways to see if such changes took place. There were changes, but scientists were not certain that these changes were evidence of life. Nothing was detected in the soil that contained carbon, which is essential to life as we know it. The surface of Mars may be more interesting than that of our Moon, but Mars still seemed to be a dead world.

The surface of Mars looks like a rocky desert similar to those found on Earth. The *Viking* probes scooped samples of Martian soil for testing. None of the tests showed definite signs of life as we know it.

Above: The Martian horizon as photographed by the *Viking* lander.
The lower center of this image shows marks left by the lander's sampling tools.

Another view of
Mars from the
Viking lander.

Martian moons. Deimos (*top*) orbits Mars in about 30 hours. Phobos (*bottom*) orbits Mars in about 7 hours and 40 minutes.

Above: Pictures taken by *Viking 1* were combined to create this image of Phobos. The craters were probably caused by the impact of space debris.

Captured Moons

Mars has two small moons, or satellites, called Phobos and Deimos. They may be captured asteroids — asteroids that were once passing Mars and were drawn into orbit by Mars's gravitational field. They are not large globes like our own Moon. From Earth, the moons look like two dim dots of light, but probes have shown them more clearly. They are shaped like potatoes and are covered with craters. At their longest points, Phobos is about 17 miles (27 km) across, and Deimos is just 9 miles (15 km) across. These little satellites were not discovered until 1877 because of their small size and their closeness to Mars. This was long after the more distant, but larger, satellites of Jupiter and Saturn were discovered.

Right: An artist's interpretation of the 1989 Soviet *Phobos* mission. One of the mission's goals was to drop a lander on Phobos to map its surface and subsurface and to study this moon's composition.

If at first you don't succeed . . .

The Martian moons were discovered by an American astronomer named Asaph Hall. Night after night in 1877, he looked through his telescope at the space near Mars and could find nothing. Finally, he made up his mind that it was no use. He told his wife, whose maiden name was Stickney, that he was giving up. His wife said, "Try it one more night." He did and found the moons. Now the largest crater on the moon Phobos is named "Stickney" in honor of the woman who urged Hall not to give up.

Getting Back to Mars

Spacecraft exploration of Mars began in the early 1960s. Numerous missions were launched, but most ended in failure – some spacecrafts did not even manage to leave, or even reach, Earth orbit. A few spectacular successes, such as *Mariner 9* and the two *Viking* missions, produced tens of thousands of pictures. After the *Vikings*, no launches were sent to Mars for over a decade.

Humans started new efforts to reach Mars in the late 1980s, but the first successful missions did not arrive at the planet until some two decades after the *Vikings*. One of those missions was *Mars Pathfinder*, which landed on the surface on July 4, 1997. It released a roving robot vehicle, called *Sojourner*, that carried out some geological studies. The mission also produced remarkable pictures. Another success was the probe *Mars Global Surveyor*, assigned to do mapping work. It was actually launched a month before *Pathfinder*, but it did not go into orbit around Mars until September 1997. Its findings included evidence that a massive flood had swept through one area of Mars as recently as perhaps 10 million years ago.

A stunning panoramic view produced by *Pathfinder*.

Above: A NASA picture of the *Sojourner* rover that was a part of the *Pathfinder* mission.

Mars Global Surveyor.

Right: This rock is called the Yogi rock, because it reminded astronomers of a big and friendly bear, like the cartoon character Yogi Bear.

A scorecard of the missions to Mars that succeeded in making it beyond Earth orbit. So far, our exploration of the Red Planet has had mixed success.

Probe	Launched	Country*	Mission Summary
Mars 1	1962	U.S.S.R.	Failure: Probe failed before reaching Mars.
Mariner 3	1964	U.S.	Failure: Batteries died shortly after launch.
Mariner 4	1964	U.S.	Success! Mars flyby.
Zond 2	1964	U.S.S.R.	Failure: Radio failed. Probe did pass Mars.
Mariner 6	1969	U.S.	Success! Mars flyby.
Mariner 7	1969	U.S.	Success! Mars flyby.
Mariner 8	1971	U.S.	Failure: Booster failed. Never reached orbit.
Mariner 9	1971	U.S.	Success! First to orbit Mars. First close-up images of Mars's moons.
Mars 2	1971	U.S.S.R.	Failure: Lander crashed on Mars.
Mars 3	1971	U.S.S.R.	Failure: Probe landed on Mars but stopped sending signals after just 90 seconds.
Mars 4	1973	U.S.S.R.	Failure: Reached Mars but failed to enter orbit.
Mars 5	1973	U.S.S.R.	Success! Returned images similar to those from *Mariner 9*.
Mars 6	1973	U.S.S.R.	Failure: Lander crashed.
Mars 7	1973	U.S.S.R.	Failure: Lander missed Mars.
Viking 1	1975	U.S.	Success! First images of Martian surface. Chemical analysis of soil. Search for life.
Viking 2	1975	U.S.	Success! First detection of earthquake on Mars. Mission similar to that of *Viking 1*.
Phobos 1	1988	U.S.S.R.	Failure: First attempt to land probes on Martian moon Phobos. Probe failed before reaching Mars.
Phobos 2	1988	U.S.S.R.	Failure: Signals ceased one week before Phobos landing.
Mars Observer	1992	U.S.	Failure: Contact lost just before achieving Mars orbit.
Mars Global Surveyor	1996	U.S.	Success! Orbiter, science mapping mission.
Mars Pathfinder	1996	U.S.	Success! Lander with rover vehicle that explored area around landing site.
Nozomi (Planet-B)	1998	Japan	Uncertain: Arrival delayed to 2004 because of propulsion problem.
Mars Climate Orbiter	1998	U.S.	Failure: Orbiter lost on arrival.
Mars Polar Lander/Deep Space 2	1999	U.S.	Failure: Lander and descent probes lost on arrival.
Mars Odyssey	2001	U.S.	Success! Orbiter, science mapping mission.

* "U.S.S.R" refers to the former Soviet Union.

Martian Life – Found on Earth?

Although space probes have sent us amazing data and pictures from Mars since the 1960s, they failed to find evidence of life on the Red Planet. They also failed to definitely disprove that life existed there, and some scientists still wonder whether some sort of life – such as tiny microorganisms like bacteria on Earth – might lie hidden below the Martian surface. Underground, better conditions for life might exist, such as water along with warmer temperatures. It may not be possible to find out for sure until people someday actually go to Mars.

Meanwhile, a hint that life may once have existed on Mars has been found on Earth. About a dozen meteorites from Mars are known on Earth. Impacts of large meteorites probably blasted them off Mars. In 1996, scientists found that one of the Martian meteorites, which is four billion years old, contains tiny structures that look like fossils left by ancient tiny microorganisms on Earth. It could not be proved that the structures in the meteorite were really made by microorganisms, but the find fueled new debate about life on Mars.

Left: Close-up of meteorites with supposed evidence of life.

Right: NASA picture of the key Martian meteorite (Martian Meteorite ALH84001).

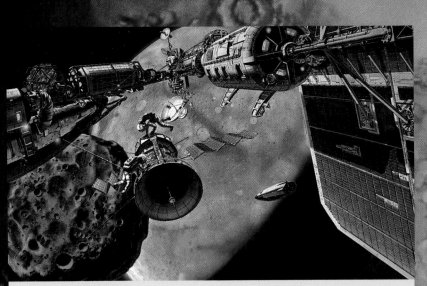

Above: A mission carrying people flies past Phobos on its way to Mars. The orbit of Phobos carries it about 6,000 miles (9,600 km) above the surface of the Red Planet.

To explorers stationed on Phobos, Mars would loom large and red.

Futuristic Colonies

Sending people to Mars on a spaceship will not be an easy task. It might take nearly two years for such a mission to return to Earth. If people do someday travel to Mars, they could build colonies.

We can imagine colonies on the Moon, because the Moon is only a three-day rocket travel-time away from Earth. Mars is much farther away, but in some ways, it would be an easier world to live on than our Moon. Mars has a gravitational pull that is $2/5$ that of Earth, while the Moon's is only $1/6$ that of Earth. Mars has a thin atmosphere that can protect people a little from meteors and radiation, but the Moon has none. Mars seems to have water below its surface, while the Moon does not. Cities could be built underground on Mars or perhaps under domes on the planet's surface.

Above: A colony on Mars would have an artificial environment — inside buildings, space suits, and vehicles — making the Martian atmosphere fit for humans. Landing at the colony would be easy enough, and the rocket launch site would allow people to leave as well.

Objects of Exploration

Once settlements are established on Mars, exploration parties can be sent out. Imagine the explorers in special cars, driving along the bottom of a canyon that stretches for 2,500 miles (4,000 km). Imagine a party climbing a giant volcano and studying the inside of the crater. Think of explorers making their way across the ice caps at the planet's poles. We know the ice caps contain frozen carbon dioxide as well as frozen water, but we could learn even more about Mars from the ice caps. We might find interesting minerals or even matter that will help us understand what Mars was like millions or billions of years ago.

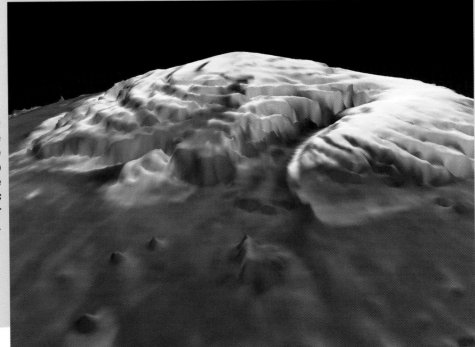

Right: A NASA 3D visualization of the Martian north pole made with the help of data from the spacecraft *Mars Global Surveyor* in 1998.

The moons of Mars — a clue to life on Earth?

Phobos and Deimos do not look like Mars. Mars has a light reddish surface, but Phobos and Deimos have dark surfaces. That may be because the two moons were probably once asteroids. Certain dark meteorites occasionally land on Earth. They contain small amounts of water and carbon-containing compounds that somewhat resemble those found in living things. Maybe it would be more interesting to study the surfaces of Mars's moons than to study Mars. This might help us investigate how life originated on Earth.

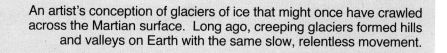

An artist's conception of glaciers of ice that might once have crawled across the Martian surface. Long ago, creeping glaciers formed hills and valleys on Earth with the same slow, relentless movement.

Above: When human beings land on Mars, they can explore the insides of inactive volcanoes like this one — the Hecates Tholus Lava Tube.

Here is a hot idea for the future: If we altered the climate and atmosphere of Mars by terraforming, we could melt the northern ice cap to help create an ocean.

Terraforming Mars

Even more exciting activities might be possible on Mars. The early settlers on Mars might be able to alter certain conditions to make the planet more like Earth. This is called terraforming. Water might be obtained from below the surface or from the asteroids. If the right gases were added to the atmosphere, Mars would trap more sunlight and become warmer. In that case, the water would not freeze and an ocean would form. Enough oxygen might be added to make the air breathable. Many plants and animals could then be brought to Mars. It may take many, many years, but perhaps Mars can someday become a little Earth.

Above: On a terraformed Mars, humans would not have to depend on artificial devices to breathe, keep warm or cool, or supply themselves with water. The terraformed climate would sustain human life "naturally."

The Sun and its Solar System
(*left to right*): Mercury, Venus,
Earth, Mars, Jupiter, Saturn,
Uranus, Neptune, Pluto.

Two Moons of Mars

Name	Diameter	Distance from Mars's Center
Phobos	11.4–16.7 miles (18.4–26.8 km)	5,827 miles (9,378 km)
Deimos	6.5–9.3 miles (10.4–15.0 km)	14,577 miles (23,459 km)

Mars versus Earth

Planet	Diameter*	Rotation Period (length of day)	Period of Orbit around Sun (length of year)	Known Moons	Surface Gravity	Distance from Sun (nearest–farthest)	Least Time for Light to Reach Earth
Mars	4,222 miles (6,794 km)	24 hours, 37 minutes	687 days (1.88 years)	2	0.38**	128–155 million miles (207–249 million km)	3 minutes
Earth	7,927 miles (12,756 km)	23 hours, 56 minutes	365.256 days (1 year)	1	1.00**	91.3–94.4 million miles (147–152 million km)	–

* Diameter at the equator.

** Multiply your weight by this number to find out how much you would weigh on this planet.

Above: A close-up of Mars and its two tiny satellites, Phobos *(left, top)* and Deimos *(left, bottom).*

Fact File: Mars Revealed

Mars is the seventh-largest planet (Earth is fifth), the fourth-closest to the Sun, and the first planet beyond Earth's orbit. It is also the last of the "inner" group of planets, all of which lie between the Sun and what is known as the asteroid belt. Beyond the asteroid belt is the "outer" group of planets, which begins with Jupiter. Since the tilt of Mars's axis is similar to that of Earth's, and since the Martian day is almost the same length as ours, Mars has the same type of seasons as Earth. Of course, Mars is much farther from the Sun than Earth is, so Mars has a longer year than we do. Its seasons are much longer, and its temperatures are much colder than Earth's.

More Books about Mars

Destination: Mars. Seymour Simon (Morrow Junior)

DK Space Encyclopedia. Nigel Henbest and Heather Couper (DK Publishing)

Is There Life on Mars? Dennis Brindell Fradin (Simon & Schuster)

Living on Mars: Mission to the Red Planet. Michael D. Cole (Enslow)

Mars. Robin Kerrod (Lerner)

Martian Fossils on Earth?: The Story of Meteorite ALH 84001. Fred Bortz (Millbrook)

The Mystery of Mars. Sally Ride and Tam O'Shaughnessy (Crown)

CD-ROMs and DVDs

CD-ROM: *Exploring the Planets.* (Cinegram)

DVD: *Mars: The Red Planet.* (DVD International)

Web Sites

The Internet is a good place to get more information about Mars. The web sites listed here can help you learn about the most recent discoveries, as well as those made in the past.

Life on Mars. www.fas.org/mars/

Mars Exploration. mars.jpl.nasa.gov/

Mars Explorer. www-pdsimage.wr.usgs.gov/PDS/public/mapmaker/

Nine Planets. www.nineplanets.org/mars.html

Views of the Solar System. www.solarviews.com/eng/mars.htm

Windows to the Universe. www.windows.ucar.edu/tour/link=/mars/mars.html

Places to Visit

Here are some museums and centers where you can find a variety of space exhibits.

American Museum of Natural History
Central Park West at 79th Street
New York, NY 10024

Canada Science and Technology Museum
1867 St. Laurent Boulevard
Science Park
100 Queen's Park
Ottawa, Ontario K1G 5A3
Canada

Henry Crown Space Center
Museum of Science and Industry
57th Street and Lake Shore Drive
Chicago, IL 60637

National Air and Space Museum
Smithsonian Institution
7th and Independence Avenue SW
Washington, DC 20560

Odyssium
11211 142nd Street
Edmonton, Alberta T5M 4A1
Canada

Scienceworks Museum
2 Booker Street
Spotswood
Melbourne, Victoria 3015
Australia

Glossary

asteroids: very small "planets." Hundreds of thousands of them exist in our Solar System. Most of them orbit the Sun between Mars and Jupiter.

atmosphere: the gases surrounding a planet, star, or moon.

axis: the imaginary straight line around which a planet, star, or moon turns.

canal: a river or waterway made by people. It was once thought that dark, narrow markings seen on Mars were canals built by Martians to move water from the ice caps to the desert areas.

carbon dioxide: a heavy, colorless gas. When humans and other animals breathe, they exhale carbon dioxide.

craters: holes on planets and moons created by volcanic activity or the impact of meteorites.

desert: a waterless area on land. Mars is often considered a desert planet.

gravity: the force that causes celestial objects to be attracted to one another.

Hubble Space Telescope: an artificial satellite containing a telescope and related instruments that was placed in orbit around Earth in 1990.

ice cap: a cover of permanent ice at either or both poles of a planet. Mars has ice caps at both poles.

Mars: the ancient Roman god of war and the name of a planet in our Solar System.

mass: the quantity or amount of matter in an object.

meteorite: a meteoroid when it hits the ground.

meteoroid: a lump of rock or metal drifting through space. Meteoroids can be as large as small asteroids, or they can be as small as specks of dust.

moon: a small body in space that moves in an orbit around a larger body. A moon is said to be a satellite of the larger body. Mars has two moons.

NASA: the National Aeronautics and Space Administration. The government space agency in the United States.

Olympus Mons: a huge, extinct volcano on Mars.

planet: one of the bodies that revolves around our Sun. Earth and Mars are planets.

Red Planet: a name that is sometimes used for Mars.

Solar System: the Sun with the planets and all the other bodies, such as asteroids, that orbit the Sun.

Sun: our star and the provider of the energy that makes life possible on Earth.

terraforming: a way of making a planet suitable for human life.

Valles Marineris: an enormous canyon on Mars.

Viking 1* and *2: probes, each with an orbiter and a lander, which touched down on Mars.

Index

Born in 1920, Isaac Asimov came to the United States as a young boy from his native Russia. As a young man, he was a student of biochemistry. In time, he became one of the most productive writers the world has ever known. His books cover a spectrum of topics, including science, history, language theory, fantasy, and science fiction. His brilliant imagination gained him the respect and admiration of adults and children alike. Sadly, Isaac Asimov died shortly after the publication of the first edition of *Isaac Asimov's Library of the Universe.*

The publishers wish to thank the following for permission to reproduce copyright material: front cover, 3, NASA and the Hubble Heritage Team (STScI/AURA); 4, United States Geological Survey; 5, NASA/JPL; 6, Jet Propulsion Laboratory; 7 (both), Lowell Observatory; 8-9, NASA; 9, Jet Propulsion Laboratory; 10, NASA; 11 (large), © John Foster 1988; 11 (inset), 12 (upper), United States Geological Survey; 12 (lower), © John Waite 1987; 13, 14, NASA; 15 (upper), National Space Science Data Center; 15 (lower), 16 (large), NASA; 16 (inset), Jet Propulsion Laboratory; 17, © Michael Carroll 1987; 18, National Space Science Data Center; 18-19, 19 (upper), NASA/JPL; 19 (lower), National Space Science Data Center; 21 (both), NASA; 22 (large), © MariLynn Flynn 1985; 22 (inset), © Paul Dimare 1985; 23, © Ron Miller 1987; 24, NASA; 25 (left), © Michael Carroll 1987; 25 (right), © MariLynn Flynn 1987; 26, © Michael Carroll 1985; 27, © Julian Baum 1988; 28-29 (all), © Sally Bensusen 1987.